# NO MERCY

## ALESSANDRO MANZETTI

Let the world know:
#IGotMyCLPBook!

**Crystal Lake Publishing**
**www.CrystalLakePub.com**

Edited by:
Jodi Renée Lester

Cover Art:
Daniele Serra

Illustrations:
Giampaolo Frizzi

Layout:
Lori Michelle—www.theauthorsalley.com

Proofread by:
Paula Limbaugh

*"The Ghost Subway" was published in the anthology *HWA
Poetry Showcase* vol. 3 (2016)

# OTHER BOOKS BY ALESSANDRO MANZETTI

*Eden Underground*

# OTHER POETRY COLLECTIONS BY CRYSTAL LAKE PUBLISHING

*Eden Underground* by Alessandro Manzetti

*Brief Encounters with My Third Eye* by Bruce Boston

*Visions of the Mutant Rain Forest* by Bruce Boston and Robert Frazier

Or check out other Crystal Lake Publishing books (http://www.crystallakepub.com/book-table/) for your Dark Fiction, Horror, Suspense, and Thriller needs, and join our newsletter while you're there.

# PRAISE FOR NO MERCY

"*No Mercy* offers the reader an extravaganza of bizarre visionary narratives embellished by a veritable cascade of surreal imagery from the pen of a master wordsmith. Recommended to be taken in small doses like a powerful hallucinogenic drug, these poems are as potent and intense as your worst nightmares and wildest dreams. Not for the faint of heart or mind."

—Bruce Boston,
SFPA Grandmaster, author of *Surrealities.*

"Manzetti's poems inspire a transcendent reality, a dream reality that slips in and out of nightmares; earthscape ruled by sensory overload, soul underload and imagination that melts into hunger for love, life and music. I loved this unearthly and yet strangely familiar meal laid before my eyes."

—Linda D. Addison,
award-winning author of
*How to Recognize a Demon Has Become Your Friend*

"What a feast of a collection! Marvelous, powerful work! Manzetti fills his canvases with broken souls —such as Janis Joplin, Frida Kahlo whose lives left footprints in our history. He introduces you to others with inspiring imagery, giving the reader much to ponder. Simply outstanding, five stars!"

—Marge Simon,
Bram Stoker Award winner

# TABLE OF CONTENTS

I dedicate this book to Janis Joplin,
even though I wrote these poems
listening to *Kind of Blue* by Miles Davis.

# THE PEARL

October 4, 1970

Alcohol and Hollywood.
The futuristic stilt house, its windows too large.
The headlights of cars slam into them,
and the blurry faces of passengers
run away fast, followed by trails of their skin,
always somewhere else.
The procession of the rush
and the heroin's symphony
with a thousand movements.
The shrink's diamond ring on her finger,
her mom's artificial teeth with no one to talk to.
"Jesus!" The music in the ears,
purgatory vomiting on the red dress
and the crapper of the Landmark Motor Hotel.

The mirror, Pearl in there, appearing and disappearing.
Drifts, shards of glass, the soul moving left and right.
Then, she sticks out her tongue. "Fuck you!"
The bottle, that taste of dust and crushed ice
in her mouth, which never goes down.
The hands on the windows, the sign
and its frame of light bulbs, down in the street.
Purgatory is full as usual.
Bessie Smith's Packard hitting the truck,
her arm torn off,
the ambulance,
a tramp who's pissing himself.

Always the same scene in her head
when the ghost comes,
that golden bitch with its big tits,
beautiful as she will never be.
Now it's in the mirror, laughing.
But come on, this isn't a real crapper,
it's full of people in there, of borderless memories.
Black out, emergency lights, the ghost lifts its dress
and shows Janis its panties stained with blood.
Thirteen years. Port Arthur.
The thorny coat of adolescence,
the smell of the river and summer,
a bra that's too big.
The ghost is bringing Janis backward,
where it hurts. "Fuck you!"

The blood that drives the wrong way,
closed eyes, which see farther,
the shapes of the last line, there.
An infinite Texas,
a Nirvana of motionless beaks of oil wells
in a land of intermittent shadows.
Black out, emergency lights.
The carpet on her face and life dripping on the shells of slee-
ping mites.
No one else knows a thing.

# FRIDA'S MONSTER

September 17, 1925

The iron monster, Xochimilco,
was waiting for me round the bend
with electric wires instead of hair,
and his long, curled tail
nailed to the asphalt like a rail.
When he saw me with my strawberry necklace,
eighteen years around my neck,
so red and soft, so delicious,
he shouted and whistled,
screeching on the road with his nails.

So, he stared at me for five seconds,
while he ate a big peach,
or maybe a woman's severed yellow head.
Xochimilco turned his eyes,
his headlights, his square muzzle,
toward the San Juan Market,
then he started looking at my dress again,
scattered with red euphorbia flowers,
and the rod between his legs,
a giant erection, a steel pipe,
a handrail for dozens of hands.

*You are mine*, he whispers in my ear,
stretching his rusty tongue through the window
of my still-intact youth,
only crossed by the sun, so far,

and touched by the colorful parrots
of a virgin imagination
and by the fast drumming-fingers
of curious monkeys
who want to taste my strawberries.
Then he breaks all the windows
overturning my thin-legged life,
and emptying my bag full of tomatoes,
sending them rolling on the floor,
through the blood of other victims,
of the monster who strikes without looking,
blind and drunk as fate.

I'm surrounded by red, liquid and solid,
Xochimilco scratches my legs to get in,
and now I feel his steel pipe inside me,
squirting his warm yellow, pink, blue, green.
Filling my belly with all the colors,
which you can see in the morning
walking through the narrow streets of Coyoacán,
among the grenade-colored buildings
and their blue skeletons.

Now I'm in my bed
with all my broken bones
and I look at the ceiling;
I'm the one up there, in the mirror,
my muse,
in armor, painted with black swallows,
that clutches my torso,
and white flowers of pain
that blossom in my eyes.

# THE MAIDEN

May 30, 1431

Fire.
Joan looks at the melted sky
dripping on her like liquid heaven;
she has no more skin, no more secrets
hidden in her cage of ribs.
Wham! Thunder from whoever's enjoying it, up there,
sixty thousand feet above.
Fire.
You can see the eye of the bastard
between those dirty faces around there;
He has a tail hidden in his pants.
Fire, still.

The stake crackles and chews, cooks,
the audience drools and the virgin burns.
A cherub with his little, newborn wings,
a one hundred and eighty-pound chicken,
slips on the bastard's black orgasm.
Fire, and sperm.
Who is Joan's father?
*The Top, the Bottom or the Dead Samsara among them?*
The bearded master of lightning,
or the red-horned bastard?

No one does anything, apart from the fire.
Fire, and nothing else.
The Ruen market, with its bunches of empty heads,

the smell of leather, of sweat and people,
a ring of voices that tightens around.
Two dried branches linked to form a cross,
the Executioner who's kicking the embers,
and the heart of the maiden which doesn't burn.
A splash of holy syrup, three seconds of rain,
—some relief there—
of milk that smells of jasmine,
the compassion of an invisible saint
gushed out from unused nipples.
Fire, even more fire.
"Jesus!" A last cry, that of someone
dying at nineteen,
desperate and pure, a kick in the shins
of Mother Nature.
A warm heart in ashes, intact,
and a brand new vagina gone to hell,
in smoke along with everything else.

Shreds, piles, living and dead ropes.
The shaky shadow of a scrawny dog
stretching its muzzle, burning its tongue.
The hooves of the horses, the storm
blown by the pipes of a church organ,
Monet's ghost, a clock without hands on his wrist,
who's painting the facade of the cathedral,
now covered by Joan's skin,
like thin, pink snow.

# THE BALLROOM

The ballroom is full of people,
of souls drooling like snails,
while out there is Monday at Alton,
and the crosses of St. Mary's are off.
*Where's June?* Everyone's asking,
they want to see her before they die.
Each one needs beauty, white teeth,
the scent of mango and tropical forests,
papaya pandemics, Chichihualtzapotl's magic
before leaving that gray and square city,
with garbage instead of mangroves
and coffins that look like canoes,
and a one-way ticket.

Miles Davis's trumpet goes upstairs
—"Blue in Green"—
It's time for a slow dance, for June,
who crosses the door like a ghost,
quickly reaching the center of the hall,
twirling, following the liquid gold
sprinkled in the air from Coltrane's saxophone,
making the ruffles and the pleats
of her red dress fly, glued to that black skin,
to her African body.

People stretch their arms,
inviting her brown hair and blue braids to dance
—*Kind of Blue*—

She smiles at everyone for their last day on Earth,
with those white teeth so young,
with fingers touching her sharp cheeks,
and the tender flesh of her lips barely open.
She's the Summer, while the Winter blows out,
crumpling old newspapers, old stories
along the roads.

*Who's first?* she asks,
shaking a bracelet of shells
wrapped around her young veins.
Mr. Raymond, who never left Alton,
takes off his hat and approaches her,
making a small bow and kissing her hand
and that ring with the black stone
that shines with a new, unknown light.

June takes him in her arms,
and they start dancing, like a real couple
who has spent a lifetime together,
sharing the same grooves
on the forehead, face, and hands,
maps of the days, every Monday,
with their coasts, coves, and secrets.
June becomes Mr. Reynolds' bride,
whom he has never known.

Then her dress changes color,
and now it's black like everything else,
while with her snake tongue
she grabs from his ear
the tail of his mesmerized soul,
to snatch it away from that small kindergarten,
to swallow it like a rat
and let it slide inside her,
and then beneath the ground,
somewhere in Africa.

# BLUE GR/CE

(inspired by "Blue Grace" by Philip Lamantia)


Lady LSD, with her thin paws,
clings to the walls of my room,
painted by Blue Grace, now.
I can walk hand in hand with Henry Miller
or Marquis de Sade,
with a necklace of black diamonds
around my neck,
listening to strange stories,
like a river collecting memories from the dead
drowned there.
Blue Grace is everywhere, everyone, everything,
a muse with purple hair
and big round glasses on its nose;
Lake Texcoco with all its swallowed guts
and shell-less hearts slipped into the waters;
the luminescent sperm of a Russian poet,
frozen in the steppe;
or Versailles and all its light
and illusions.

Lady LSD kisses me with her warm tongue,
filling me with Blue Grace,
too much grace,
that of the last Tropic of Cancer,
of Bosch's paintings,
letting me see the shining black of Manet,
the tenth planet on the edge of the plate,

the Exposition Internationale du Surréalisme
in Paris, in 1938 and then in 2138.
I can walk hand in hand with Man Ray,
Marcel Duchamp, or my unborn son
in a radioactive future,
with museums full of skeletons of books,
skulls of writers and tyrannosaurus teeth.
Blue Grace, it's no longer anywhere, here
where she's dragging me by the legs,
between these blocks of ice
containing human eyes, still perfectly open
for the past hundred years at least.
What have they seen?

An apocalyptic Pompeii,
gigantic, from pole to pole,
inhabited by shadows of revolutions,
carcasses of electronic head factories
and blue eggs of asteroids.
Who are you Lady?

# THE RESURRECTION OF THE PEARL

Alcohol and Hollywood.
A futuristic stilt house with wide, watery, concrete eyes.
They observe the vertical, nervous dance of rain,
and the linear flow of cars down the road,
squirting puddles and slices of faces.
Inside those big rectangular eyes
are framed the small ones of the Pearl:
all her face that could fit inside there.

Night, heroin stars make the sky glitter,
one of them falls off and ends up around Janis's finger.
A diamond ring? But her lover doesn't exist,
he's made of acid, of the imaginary cells of nothing,
and spits whiskey from his mouth.
"Cry Baby," suggests the ghost with its head shaped like a
bottle,
pulling the sleeve of her red dress.
*Come with me*, he whispers in her ear.
A kiss that Janis immediately vomits
in the crapper of the Landmark Motor Hotel.
She raises her head, with butterflies in her hair.
Back to Port Arthur, on the banks of the river,
a trip on a rump that's too fast, without stopping.
*Fuck you, I will not come back here*, whispers the Pearl.
She dives, riding the tide until she pops out the other end,
in the hotel room.

Fourteen years later, wet;
it rains heavily out there, and it's cold now.
Her strange lover is inside her bed,
with his smooth skin and a mesmerizing mandala
tattooed on his chest.
He has syringes instead of fingers, a noose around his head,
and a golden spoon in hand
containing, in balance, a black pearl.

*Did you bring Aunt Hazel?* she asks.
*It's all up there, don't you see? Take what you want,*
replied her colorful hero.
And it's true, Janis looks the other way, for a moment,
but when her eyes turn again to the man,
she sees he's become a block of ice,
slowly melting into the bed.
Cold. Never mind, she can do it on her own,
traveling until tomorrow,
to the next sun, the next concert.
She tightens the tourniquet on her gray arm,
biting her lip.
Music, right now. "Cry Baby."
What the fuck?

Janis looks up at the ceiling.
She sees a porthole that leads somewhere else,
to another dirty hotel room,
where there is a girl on the bed,
with bloody knees and a lot of bruises
all over her just preyed-upon body,
who's breastfeeding a knife, a steel lover;
the girl's red lips are moving, whispering something.
*Is she praying or singing with me?* Janis wonders.
Maybe the music changes again in that place up there
which shows that cheap hotel.
Janis comes back to the crapper and
throws in all that shit she was going to send

straight to her eager veins.
*Bye-bye Paradise.* Music must come first, right?

She combs her hair, trying a decent smile
in front of the encrusted mirror,
then comes out of that hole
teetering on her heels, dressed for her show.
Then she grabs the microphone and starts singing
before hundreds of portholes
which now pierce that fucking room
like a termite mound:
above, below, everywhere.
That sad girl on the bed and thousands of others
are going to turn on the music, turn on Janis,
to dress their armored hope,
to dance with strawberries around their necks,
—soft red dreams—
forgetting yesterday, just here right now.

# NO MERCY

A hobo walks around the streets of Christiania,
with some pebbles to suck on in the pockets
of his long brown coat; he's hungry,
and he must have read Knut Hamsun.
He's been drifting around to the north
or maybe to the south—*who knows?*—
with his bent shoulders frozen
by the broad shadow of the Akershus Fortress,
its rectangular stomachs full of windows
and the fat of heated rooms.

Looks like his luck just ran out,
as long as he sees something shimmering
in a green plastic dumpster,
its toothless mouth wide open all night long.
If that sparkling light is an illusion of starvation,
of death in slow-motion,
dragging you into its blue house
one millimeter per day,
there is no more mercy for him, the man thinks.

The hobo approaches the treasure,
smiling with his three teeth,
the tombstones of what he was:
a man, a husband, a father.
He looks inside, resting his hands on the edges
of his magic well,
while an elderly woman,

wearing a traditional green *bunad*,
with a loaf of bread under her arm,
stops looking at him,
making the sign of the cross.
The devil with a string in place of a belt,
who killed his wife one year ago
to give birth to a deformed monster
with the same blue eyes and aquiline nose
of that man who's digging through waste,
sucking his crucifix
to satisfy his deep hunger;
that's his curse.

The man finds the hand of a woman in there,
which comes out with a fake diamond ring
wrapped around its hard index finger,
pointing to that too-white sky,
the cover that persecutes him, blinding him.
He pulls hard, but the mysterious woman
is stuck down there; he has to dig again.

He pulls out a piece of her arm,
with sturdy bones, gray, greasy,
from under a moldy mattress
covered in a shroud of desperates matings
and liquid dreams: a white sunflower
up there, where there was a pillow,
the belly pierced by rat bites,
and the blood of wool which comes out like cirri;
in the middle of it, the man recognizes
the wet stripes of legs and arms wide open:
those of the chained waiting for death
or for the queen with her whip.

Digging, digging again.
Below an old plastic spaceship
and a couple of tomato jars

filled with out-of-date coins,
he can finally see her chest
below a jigsaw puzzle of used syringes
and her big breasts rising
from the plastic waterfalls on the sides,
like two giant mozzarellas.
She's a two-hundred-pound triple Venus
buried in leftovers.

Remove, move, and discover again,
freeing all that flesh.
Here she's white like a Madonna,
big as a goddess of Malta.
The hobo enters the dumpster,
locking himself in with his new bride,
to swallow all his curses,
to taste that blessing of heaven,
which is finally becoming red;
the sunset, the peace, the fat under the teeth.
Maybe it will be a night without tomorrow this time,
while white Norway is falling asleep,
forgetting all the outcasts.

# YUKI

The three strings of the sanshin and a flesh doll
who's singing "Yuki" on her toes.
But outside it's summer, there is no snow.
The closed windows,
the branches of the sun broken on the floor,
a pink *yukata* stained with cherry blossoms,
with a purple band around the waist,
dances like a little ghost
hanging on the wires of a short time:
It's a dress too large for a nine-year-old girl.

*Yuki ya konko, arare ya konko*
*futtemo futtemo zunzun tsumoru*
*yama mo nohara mo wataboshi kaburi*
*kareki nokorazu hana ga saku*

Liu, a blue silk stripe in her eyes
and so many flavors on her tongue.
*Dance for me . . .*
A black sugar candy in her mouth,
an empty glass of paradise juice,
the feeling of being out of her body,
able to observe herself
through a transparent ceiling, above.

Looking at herself from up there,
dancing with all the flowers scattered on her body,
and then seeing him darting all around.

# ALESSANDRO MANZETTI

*It's a man?* No, perhaps a tsuchinoko,
because he jumps nearby, naked, drunk,
applauding her every move.
Liu has read in fairy tales
something about that strange creature.
Like a snake, it sucks alcohol and spews lies,
capable of jumping a meter away,
and swallowing its tail to roll like a wheel.
*But where is its tail?*
And where is the snow to sing,
closed up here in this summer house?

# BLUE ARSENIC

(inspired by "Blue Like a Desert" by Joyce Mansour)


Happy are the solitary ones
those who draw faces in front of their feet
those who have inexistent friends of sand
those who do not run behind anyone
because they read the ground
and it's all they need.
Happy are the lookouts over the ocean of the desert
those who shoot mirages with a rifle
banging their colorful heads from their torso.

The sun bleeds out on the horizon
forming red puddles
between the bedridden rocks, above thirsty graves
which suck the ground like babies at the nipple.
No one knows it no one.
The sky becomes black
with a fat polar star in its center
a fixed eye which rotates capturing images:
the blind eagle returns to the nest waiting for dawn
the snake breaks the frost scales smothering the rat
a woman holds her man's shoulders
letting their navels stick.

The nomad listens to Death
passing on the gravel in front of his tent
going to grab insomnia's hair
friends and lovers of others near there;

# ALESSANDRO MANZETTI

in their ears a sad lullaby has been sounding for hours
sung by an ancient mother with a drum on her lap
with tattooed flowers on her fingers
with bluish breasts swollen with arsenic
and a hand on the rope of the guillotine near her
who knows how to cut off
Now from Elsewhere.

# THE GHOST SUBWAY

After having a few too many drinks,
some claim that in the stomach of the city,
just below Joe's Bar,
or perhaps in the cellar of the funeral store
near the corner of Steinbeck Street,
the entrance of the Ghost Subway stands,
the one with the blue wagons
decorated by the graffiti of fat pythons
and millions of photographs of black and white faces,
who carry the souls of the old ones
to the warehouse of the dead.

Some others say the driver of that Subway is Tom Joad
with Charon's brand new license in his pocket,
freed from his apartment in Hell thanks to a special permit,
and his wife, Rosa Tea,
with her ivory wedding dress and a long train,
held up by two angels with useless hen's wings,
wearing a blue T-shirt with CALIFORNIA written above,
she walks through the wagons to nurse the most tired souls
with her compassionate breasts
swollen with cyanide.

The ticket of the Ghost Subway is free
and you don't have to look for its station;
it will find you when the time comes,
when the rain fills your socks and shoes
and hundreds of snails crawl

on the edges of the old jar of your soul,
when you're too tired to die
and you need a ride to the other side, quickly
running under the belly of indifferent buildings
that don't believe in ghosts.

And then there are those who tell the story
of the poet called Route 66,
with the wool hat pulled down to his eyes
and the blue notebook in his jacket pocket,
who discovered the Ghost Subway station
before he died, before all the others,
so he travels every night in those blue wagons
taking notes, heartening the frightened souls.
He reaches the other side and goes back to the city
to sit under the arcades in the same place,
to tell a thousand stories to the bystanders
who throw pennies into his hat.

# FIVE RED DAYS

(inspired by "Five Haiku" by Paul Éluard)

A saxophone and a knife:
Coltrane is golden yellow,
the hooker on the asphalt is red.

The mute girl shouts:
The miracle of a raping
by a holy husband.

A man collects a hundred greenbacks,
the car launched runs over him
while the lady in black drinks a martini.

The last hit, a drop of blood on my arm,
and a violet, purple and orange shadow;
Janis Joplin's ghost is following me.

The Seine, undecided,
doesn't let the corpse floating on her soak;
this is not Henry Miller's Paris.

# THE MERCY OF A REPTILE

Black spring, medicine for every curse,
crawl over here, wrap around me,
let me become your favorite termite mound.
Show me your mouth of Africa,
the magnificent seven of Somalia,
the plains of the coast,
the flat miles and the tapered peaks.
Sink your teeth, take me away with you,
don't leave me here to die underground
with my brain still running,
below that wooden sky.
Find me, follow the smell of desperation.
Can you hear my knees hitting
this fucking coffin?
Can you hear my sips of carbon dioxide
and dreams swallowed like iron wires?

The black mamba listened to me,
it tightens hard on my thigh
and, like a black velvet seraph,
stretches under my skirt to kiss my belly;
one bite, the fastest way out
for all kinds of despair, of those who scream
beneath fifty inches of ground,
like me, buried alive after a honeymoon
with a hungry brigade of soldiers;
of those who cry in silence, within the head's walls,
out there, every day, hundreds of them,

strangled by a circle of drooling men,
a noose of flesh and bones,
naked, mocked, beaten for having shown their faces,
their lips so red, the apricot of their cheeks
and their large eyes of little girls,
before being stoned to death
under the blue eyes of a male God
with a thunderbolt between his golden legs.

# THE WINDOW

(inspired by "Under Cover of Night" by Robert Desnos)


Down here, on the street
still surrounded by the Oort cloud of your voice,
and by the too-tight orange halo
of a bottle of Southern Comfort,
I'm looking at the building in front of me,
our second-floor apartment, in there;
your shadow at the window is you and no one else,
it's you, with your purple dress and no shoes.
Do not open that window behind those curtains,
shut your eyes, please.
Why do you keep watching me up there?
But the window opens and the breeze, the breeze
shows me your body again,
hanging by the neck from the chandelier,
which makes you shine like a silent diamond
for all the others,
but not for me.

# ELECTRONIC DEATH

A white mandala, an electric cosmos of one,
without a center, ropes and geometries,
an ouroboros with two heads of women
who put their tongues in each other's mouths,
the salty flavor of high voltage
which slides down the throat;
the old life which tasted like glue
and the body that seemed to weigh tons.

A fiberoptic umbilical cord
and a jump into a tunnel of lights,
a kaleidoscope of pulses, enlightened
memories and virtual rose windows.
The central nave, vertical
to the cathedral of yourself,
the gothic arches of gray and stone textures,
and below the tombs of your old data.

Then finally, over there,
a girl with blue braids is found,
an avatar without blood, menses, or legs,
with a Glasgow smile across her face,
like the Black Dhalia,
who takes you by the hand
and pulls you down
through the tunnel of a fake Paradise
built by a hacker of Death.

# ALESSANDRO MANZETTI

You only have five minutes of that
to free your imagination
from an inexhaustible bladder,
extinguishing supernovae, riding toward yourself
on the back of a phosphorescent vulva
with five legs and the eight eyes of a spider
on its rose and violet muzzle,
running in a white desert,
from which sprout, like cactus,
the heads of what you've always hated,
that you can chop off with your axe of restoration.
You can taste all those megabytes of Eden,
that electronic caviar that was prepared for you
thanks to the system's backdoor.
You're a virus, right now.

A white mandala, an orgasm of one,
without walls of flesh and muscles.
A heretic ouroboros, your head that bites the tail of a virgin,
who smells the way you like it, who is as you imagined;
her dunes and Raffaello's perfect lines
and the crooked horizon of her pelvis
where you tie the dawn of your sperm,
which drips red and orange
on her polished belly,
waiting for the death of the pink of her skin.

Then you find in your hands
a slingshot, which lets you
throw the seeds of people,
as many as you want, in that still empty land;
The first green plants, the blossoms of your creations
with flesh petals, corollas of breasts and byzantine buttocks,
which start walking right next to the hectares
of what you have buried, hidden,
in the white ground, there, below silicon crosses
where there are tombs of passwords

dug by the hungry dogs
of the hard disk that wants to swallow everything
in its rectangular stomach.

A white mandala, a journey of one,
without motors or sore bones, without shoes;
an impossible ouroboros with a hundred heads and tails,
a concentric maze, the green texture of Buxus
and the regular hedgerows.
The testicles of rounded bushes and endless turns.
Your doors, your corners,
and then back and forth, holding strong
to the rope of forever,
the threads untangled, once and for all.

A white mandala, a journey of one,
without motors or sore bones, without shoes;
an impossible ouroboros with a hundred heads and tails,
a concentric maze, the green texture of buscus
and the regular hedges of circuits
surrounding the motherboard
and its processor that looks like
the black monolith of the *Planet of the Apes*.
Satisfied like a greedy electron,
and making the paws to your brain grow,
you can define yourself a Brain God, native,
powerful, like the centrifugal orbits of Astabek II.
But you have consumed your five minutes,
and the system re-engages its floating avatar.
The girl with blue braids smiles,
then she makes a strange grimace from ear to ear,
raises her electric saw, and cuts you in two
like herself.
DELETED.

# YUKI'S MONSTER

Liu stays back, at a distance.
She wants to see how it ends.
It's better not to go back in there,
into that little girl's body.
Juice of paradise, aroma of apple and butter.
All you need is one sip
and you can get out through the navel,
tight as a reed.
*Looking at you for the first time. Isn't it funny?*
You should try it.

But then the tsuchinoko is swollen with blood
and begins to undress its flesh doll,
pulling away her *yukata*, rubbing it between its fingers,
on its reddened face,
letting her newborn breasts dance
on the bed with blue silk sheets,
which seem like a crumpled sky.
The claws on her knees, the breath of alcohol,
the lies hidden between her legs
like dirty snow.
Trails of saliva on that almost new skin, so elastic,
the bruises of too-large hands
and, there in the middle,
drops of blood evaporating
along with her twelve years.

Looking from up there
and having to close her eyes,
just like those spilled on the bed,
clenched by a strip of blue.
The strange creature leaves
the immobile girl, gasping;
there is no more music,
and all the cherry blossoms on her *yukata*,
unsewn, are falling to the floor.
Snow inside and outside,
turning summer into winter, suddenly.
It can really happen.

The tsuchinoko gets dressed; it doesn't jump now;
it feels a noise, like a cracking,
looks upward and sees the other Liu,
the illusion on the transparent ceiling
that is spying on him;
she moves her hands from her face,
and through that little slit between her fingers
she recognizes the creature:
*Dad, so young, damn him.*

Memory blends cards and faces like a cheater,
and that infamous tsuchinoko really does . . .
eat its tail and roll like a wheel,
making the same scene reappear
a hundred, a thousand times,
rewinding the past
and tying the present in knots, twenty years later;
Liu, in front of the mirror,
a vertical transparent ceiling
glued to life, above and below.

\*\*\*

Okinawa. Seven years later.
A man hung on a cherry tree,

screwed by the past that comes back
bigger and stronger:
an angry daughter together with a monster,
a weird friend of hers.
A deadly couple.
The tsuchinoko hung on a cherry tree,
feeding a puddle of green blood;
a circle broken forever.
This time, the illusion of the creature
doesn't work.

A man hung, dead,
with his pants down at his ankles.
No more fairy tales,
powder of flies, still summer . . .
like that first time.
Liu stretches out her arm
and pushes her father's carcass,
making it swing back and forth,
just as he came and left, every night,
her bedroom.
That close face, now so distant,
then a horrible swinging of images,
of accelerations, zooming into his flesh.

Monster's iron fists continue to slaughter
the already dead flesh of the man,
sinking like crazy pistons
in the bowels of that hanging body.
Then its long nails dig inside the belly
searching for something . . .
*It's useless*, thinks Liu;
his rotten soul is no longer
in there.
Her monster didn't have to kill him so soon,
so she makes it return to her navel,
inside herself, safe;

she no longer needs its rage,
its own rage,
seven feet high, with long fangs
and the shining blue skin
of psychosis.

"Don't look at me that way," Liu whispers
turning her eyes to the right,
toward her childhood home.
"I know what you're thinking, but I don't care."
Flies and mosquitoes,
the frustration of the death of the sun
and the red snow on the lawn,
under the tree and the window
of that room without light,
where the bleeding head of a woman appears,
crowned with glass splinters
and crack necklaces.

Looks like a sculpture, her mother
messed up that way,
with a frozen scream engraved
on the massacred face,
half-sliced, chopped,
like something passed through a meat grinder
with broken teeth.
Her eyes wide open, a flower in her mouth,
white like her silence.

"All you can do is watch me?"
she shouts at her mother,
thrown against the window
by the monster that lives in her belly.
But she can't answer Liu,
they seem to say, two shadows
at the sides of the woman's corpse,
shaking their heads and thin horns.

Liu holds her head in her hands,
crushing slimy memories,
making them escape from her ears
like black snails.
Then she smells death around her,
its aroma of honey and fig jam,
of cigars and turpentine,
of tea and pine bark, wind and closed boxes,
of cellar and midday, clean sheets and sperm.
Death, which has so many different flavors.
Death hanging on the tree, crosses its eyes.
Death which resigns, lying in the bed
of that room without windows,
looks at its bare feet and smiles.
Nothing else.

# A DREAM OF MILK AND BLOOD

Mr. Grillet closes his eyes
and sees a padded red leather door,
covered with small glass rhombuses
that don't reflect anything;
all you need is to get close,
to already be on the other side.
*Jesus Christ, but what . . . what . . .*
Mr. Grillet stutters, jaw dropping,
the last words fall from his lips,
crashing into crumbs around his bare feet.
*But where are my shoes? And my toes?*

What the man is seeing now
is nothing but the staircase of an old palace,
with an ancient wrought-iron spaceship in the middle:
the intricate cage of an elevator,
its sliding door a metal bellows
decorated with sharp bay leaves,
clanking back and forth, inviting him to enter.

Mr. Grillet, hesitant,
crosses the threshold of that strange cage
for birds without wings,
which promises to take him to Paradise.
However, he needs a coin
to start the elevator and discover his destination.
The man searches in his jacket pockets

and finds something tinkling at his fingertips:
A ten-cent piece from 1963,
bronze and aluminum,
with the engraving: *Liberté, Égalité, Fraternité.*

Mr. Grillet looks at those coins
instead of Marianne's profile, with her hair in the wind,
the French Republic in flesh, bones, and tits;
the rough face of his father appears,
the mustachioed collector who spent hours
cleaning his fucking antique coins.
*You, bastard . . . even here?*

The elevator swallows the coin
through its narrow bronze slit
like a thin, hungry Charon,
and suddenly starts, sinking into the bowels of the building.
The yellow light of the lamp explodes,
freeing a dense dark between the wet walls
of that infinite concrete groove
that runs like a train toward the lower floors,
passing them quickly, one after the other,
making the lit doorframes run uphill
as if they had a rocket tied to their backs.

The brakes of the flying cage are glowing
the same sparkles of a sad New Year's Day,
a sharp midnight of the past
awakened in the mind of Mr. Grillet,
who is held at the bars with his skin drawn upward
from the suction cup of speed.
*Jesus Christ, stop . . . stop, please!*
The light turns on again
and the elevator slows down, creaking,
with its wrought-iron floral decorations
warped, incandescent.
Mr. Grillet raises his eyes to the ceiling of the cabin,

and bites his lips until they bleed . . .
*Hell, this is just a damn hell.*

He saw that it isn't the lamp light now, up there,
but a big nipple from which
torrents of whitish liquid begin to gush,
like a living fire-fighting system.

Mr. Grillet, with his stomach in his throat
and his bowels twisted like a candy cane,
can take in his hands some drops
of that dense stuff that is dripping
from the luminous areola above him;
he tastes it, dipping his finger . . . *it's milk* . . .
it's filling the cabin and won't escape
through the openings and metal grids:
it remains there, against all logic,
and the level rises more and more.

Mr. Grillet feels the cold, pasty milk,
gurgling on his lips . . .
*No, no one can die twice. So where am I now?*
Then a face emerges suddenly in front of him,
a rancid, half-eaten face
decorated with tufts of red hair and algae braids,
with two stones buried in its orbits
and a moray eel nestled in the throat,
which bites the air, just above the surface
of that milky mass spreading over both.
*No, you're not . . . Mom. You're coming from down there,*
*right?*

But there is no time for a response,
the moray eel, the new tongue of the woman,
charging the springs of its slimy coils,
dotted with small purple balls,
snaps to attack the man,

but the cabin arrives at the end of its race,
crashing at 120 miles an hour
on the hump of the slope.
The cage crashes, deforms,
folds down on itself like a steel leghold trap.
The hideous creature, back from the sea,
where it had been buried alive,
screams with laurel leaves and wrought-iron spears
stuck inside the eyes,
grinding bubbles and dissolving into a whirlwind of milk.

The elevator widens hips in an obscene way
and spits out all the damn liquid,
together with the body of Mr. Grillet
who slips inside that white current
like a whirling tadpole
until rolling in a dry, warm place
and slamming face-first into an old Persian carpet.
Then, he raises his eyes to see:
A poor furnished room in front of him,
and the silhouette of a nude man,
whose purple skin is decorated with thick veins,
who handles coins,
drooling all over them, giggling.

That kind of monster has a transparent belly,
inside it there is an orange liquid eldorado.
Southern Comfort, the same color,
the same sparkling glow of an anger so ancient.
Those bottles in a row, half empty,
on the table in the kitchen . . .
when Mr. Grillet was nine years old,
that was his usual landscape.
Then, behind his father's dirty tank top,
he sees a smaller face beaten to a pulp,
that red hair, the sadness and fear on her lap,
two invisible monkeys that pull down

her lips and the corners of her mouth.
And yes, she absolutely is
his mother, still alive, in a hot, dry place.

The Coltrane saxophone playing,
the creaking spine of his father,
of the springs of the double bed,
the statuette of the Virgin Mary
with a blue mantle on her shoulders
and a porcelain tear on her cheek.
That is the home of his childhood;
this must be Purgatory or Hell;
this is where the elevator brought him,
Mr. Grillet thinks.

The monster, the anarchist mutation of his father,
turns and stares at that man, his son
still floating on the marble floor.
The he gets up from the chair grunting,
and approaches him with his stomach
full of orange eldorado.
He kneels before his son,
watches him as a curious animal,
with his horse eyes and flies buzzing in his closed mouth;
he touches his hair, then grabs him by the jaw,
pulls a ten-cent coin from his pants
and inserts it into a thin slot on Mr. Grillet's forehead.
*A cold crash in the brain.*

Memories come back all together, lined up in the front row,
like a long frost, a napalm of snow that covers everything,
preserving what has passed, forgotten,
under the ground and under the water.
The sea, that day, fishing all together,
the bucket full of eels
and the heart that pinches of happiness, for once;
the smiling mother with red hair in the wind,

who empties the orange bottle in the sand.
*What were you thinking, bitch, doing this?*
The puddle dries while she spits blood everywhere
with her skull split in two . . .
by a stick encrusted with fossils and cerebral matter
next to her, tight in his father's hands,
who now is dragging her by the feet along the shore,
to the rotten pier,
and the sun that is floating down there.
A stone tied to her neck,
and the moray eels waiting for fresh food
in their underwater holes.

After the crash of memories,
Mr. Grillet's chest starts to open slowly.
The coin of the Monster has worked fine.
His flesh slides away, his muscles let go of their grip,
and his ribs are rising;
his chest opens like the shell of a mollusc
until the heart shows, there in the middle,
and continues to beat without a shield.

The monster opens its mouth, drooling,
releasing the flock of white flies
imprisoned between its curved fangs,
which fly away suddenly
in an explosion of dust.
Mr. Grillet can't move now.
He feels the fast-paced bites of his father,
up and down, inside his open, disarmed chest . . .
tongue slips like a brush,
licking the juice between his heart's valves,
and those old lips sucking his ventricles,
murmuring, during the short breaks:
*Delicious.*

# MORNING SUICIDE

(inspired by "Greenwich Village Suicide" by Gregory Corso)


She draws her uterus on the window;
it looks like a fat cross,
or an orchestra leader
seen from behind,
bent to receive the applause
of his audience,
or the head of an alien
with tentacle flakes on the sides.
Then she looks down
thinking of Klimt,
his *Three Ages of Woman*
envying the mother in the middle
with flowers in her hair
and a ghost of herself in her arms
[when she was a child].
She falls,
they take her away with a pregnancy test
still tight in her hands,
and a storekeeper throws hot water
on the sidewalk.

# APOCALYPTIC MASS

I'm the last man in this city,
maybe even beyond,
but I've never seen that beyond,
beyond these walls guarded by big rats,
with their toothed minefields.
Beyond any pain, they are there, the beasts:
rats, so many, with their phosphorescent veins
(and their rabid queen).
They're viruses with four paws
of shit rebelling against their solitude,
against their infinite deadlock,
becoming a force, an army,
beyond the worst predictions,
just before of the explosion
of the Apocalypse's pipelines.

An impossible, electric rattle is chasing me,
it comes a long way; it can jump on the bridges
and arrive in a second on the other side, beyond;
its sound seems like that of chewed flesh,
of a ceiling of welded insects,
and turns the crank of an eternal soundtrack,
a song stuck in the mind of a buried memory.
*If you wear that velvet dress.*
It resonates inside the Gothic necks of churches,
blowing in holy horns,
swelling the bladder of the squares,
and then becomes a large womb,
a tide, beyond again,

then a pulsing shore and an elastic horizon
which growls at the yellow and gray of the suburbs,
splashing heretical colors
and underworld's vitriol
on blank billboards.
Then it reaches me, every time,
in the bottleneck of myself, in the blind alley,
stopping on the damned roof
on which the sunset light burns,
entangled between satellite dishes
which hear the remote sound of death.

I'm a black spot in the lens
of a rusty telescope,
a black hole in the walls of gaunt hamlets;
I'm imprisoned in a videogame,
in the seventh level, between flashing icons
and fire-breathing dragons.
I'm a fly under an upside-down glass,
I can't run away, with no beyond;
I have to stop and wait for it.
My madness shows its magenta breasts,
it twists its neck, cracking the bones,
it takes off her panties, slipping them over
feet too white and too thin,
and then it comes inside me, and beyond.

I don't feel anything beyond my madness,
it smells of bleach,
of a parade of dead sunflowers and moldy hives
pulsating in empty rooms.
It enters my nest, taking out space between my ribs.
She gets small and sharp, lifts my liver,
and makes confetti of guts with her transmarine nails,
then digs under, inside me, and beyond.
It's installing itself, I feel it,
and at the same time Calypso,

the ghost that lives beyond the edges,
opens her eyes.
In a macabre brooch in her red hair she has
the skeleton of the first mutated rat.
I'm her now, and the city is suddenly too small, empty.
Big rats tow my hunting chariot,
holding steel cables between their teeth.
The shimmering harpoon is ready,
I would like nothing more, beyond,
than to throw it into the flesh of the last man,
of the next city of this vast planetary landfill,
hit by asteroid Ybyi 21.
Apocalypse always needs a hand,
a collision, a bastard son of megatons,
to light the fuse and go farther.

***

The coast moves away behind us,
behind the survivors.
Asunción cradles her daughter without a head;
she sings something with her tight mouth
and burnt lips,
Mauricio engraves a blood mermaid on his skin
with the brilliant blade of a machete,
Catalina is knotting her intestines,
making a nice ribbon of flesh, distractedly.

The island appears, down to the right,
with its long tail of boats
stuffed with man's pulp and juice of fear.
They're seeking salvation, like us,
floating on a surface of chopped human flesh;
this is the new skin of the sea, the Apocalypse's tattoo.
Hector, the old man, stands up,
he takes off her rags, pounding his chest
and blaspheming toward the new sky,
which only knows how to piss fire

and hydrochloric acid.
If it starts to rain, we'll all be screwed,
liquefied to the bone.
But Hector seems to be able to talk
with that cursed sky;
he faces it hard, maybe challenging it.
With his abnormally unscrewed jaws,
he shouts, blowing between his smashed molars
and those teeth that haven't chewed flesh for two years.
Our captain slows down the dinghy
and pushes his blue eyes into the binoculars.
Then he tells us about the island,
of what he can see
and what he wants us to imagine . . .
whispering wonders to keep us alive.
My mind returns to the mainland,
sinking my feet into the blood
of the slaughterhouse at the harbor,
where they kill each other
to take the latest rides to the island,
where the mutated make a mess of fresh meat.
They're the new gods,
those with tails and infinite stomachs,
forged by stars and sewers.

An abomination that continues to reproduce itself
through heretic, radioactive matings.
A great flood that comes from beneath the feet,
from manholes,
a dark, armed tide that rises, biting calves.
The red foam and purple blend
of the old masters of the world.

Then the hot rain, which washes all the shit,
human and other, every two hours,
leaving space for new, white highways of bones
and hair ash everywhere.

Christ. Pompei and Chernobyl,
seasoned with rats and phosphorescent blood.
Heretic and acid rainbows, as large transparent bridges,
they drive the crowds like steel balls,
in the crazy pinball machine of Planet Earth.
We all have flashing an extra to hit:
the last ride to the island,
and whoever is in the row in front of you
is your fucking enemy number one.
Ybyi 21, Year 0,6: this is the day
of our new calendar,
for those who are lucky enough
to have counted so long.

Silvanio starts to tell the story of Calypso,
the ghost of the Apocalypse;
everyone listens to him, now,
even the headless girl of Asunción
and the purple root in her neck that spits blood.
Someone has awakened Calypso,
says the fat whoremonger, massaging his beard;
he left, floating in the air,
the ruby wrapped around his little finger.
Long before the fall of the asteroid
and the Kaesŏng's kaboom, he knows it for sure.
The queen of rats and the end of things, so he calls her.
No one wants to talk, to ask questions.
Our captain has tied to his leather belt
a rosary of cut human fingers;
that's the way it was paid
to bring people to the island, to salvation.
From moment zero,
when the asteroid fucked Planet Earth in the ass,
twenty grams of non-infected proteins,
which can be solid gold.
Twenty fingers, twenty passengers, twenty survivors.
Twenty grams of protein.

\*\*\*

The alpha rat, squirming, comes out through the siphon,
shakes its wet fur and grinds its teeth
in the great *égout*, the underground highway of Paris.
Calypso, immersed up to her waist
in the gray and black waters,
is dressed as a bride and walks
toward the center of the sewer
with her ivory leather and blue veil,
and the long black train,
wet with the sperm of the Seine,
which swirls, sewn and covered by
polished cockroach shells.

The alpha rat rises on two paws,
ready to attack and defend
its filthy harem of odalisques with tails,
and the den in Gallery 18
of the Rive Gauche sewage system,
protected by a palisade of rotten human fingers.
Calypso touches the waters,
caressing the carcasses of eyeless dolls,
which slowly emerge through the surface
with their plastic bellies.

Calypso lets down her red hair,
then bends and licks her wrists,
tattooed with two red omegas,
the Apocalypse's buttons.
The alpha rat is enchanted by her beauty,
dragged by an invisible hook, inside.
It approaches her, waits for a woman's nod,
and here it is:
her tongue, which walks around
the soft corolla of her lips.
The rat dives and reaches the bare thighs
of its new odalisque without a tail.

Underwater, the alpha rat doesn't need
to see or look;
its ancestral radar, connected to its muscles' twitch,
marks bright, clear trajectories,
vibrating toward Calypso's slit,
dilated on the sides by the plastic fingers
of the dolls without eyes, buoys of pleasure,
maids of that heretic wedding.

When the alpha rat is inside of her,
Calypso's slit closes
and the trap of the oyster snaps;
the animal, sucked into her uterus, having to mate
as she wants to, quickly fertilizing her eggs
before its lungs explode for lack of air.
She looks up at the galleries, right and left,
staring at their obscene graffiti,
sprinkled with solitude:
a futuristic Noah's Ark,
with the imprint TITANIC on the hull
and four phallic fireplaces on the rump,
from which they dive, into an ocean of sperm and sharks,
billy goats with golden teeth,
surrealistic sirens with three breasts and pearls in the hair,
crowned priests,
and sons of bitches in tuxedos with triton masks.

Calypso feels that the alpha rat
did its job inside her;
after a deep breath,
she immerses a hand in the black water,
making it enter her tight slit.
Then she pulls out the prisoner,
clutches it between her nails,
raising and looking at it,
catches her breath and reconnects herself
with reality, with its reign in the égout.

# ALESSANDRO MANZETTI

She smiles at the rat,
bringing it to her mouth
before biting deep into its neck.
Calypso's tongue gets the flavor of rust,
of chestnuts and anchovies,
while she devours the alpha rat,
her husband with the tail,
the king of outflow and waste;
the sewer's tide raises its back,
galleries fill to bursting,
uncovering the shafts.

From the manholes, gusts of rotten things
hit the painted buildings,
spreading the black water across the streets;
a newborn Seine flows, heretical and black, violent,
next to the old one.
Winter, Ybyi 21 Year -0.1; it's cold,
a court of rats clings to Calypso's body,
they weld to each other, sinking their teeth,
to build a living fur,
to warm their queen.

Calypso swallows the last bite of the alpha rat,
licks its little bones, shaping them
to make a hair clip,
while the army of rats,
obsessed with the smell of its queen,
forms waves of black muscles everywhere,
which become the new skin of that drifting city.
Calypso observes the sunset over Paris;
she sees, beyond the core of that ancient purple,
beyond deep space,
the embryos of new asteroids,
every second ever closer to Earth,
full of their infected milk.

# THE END⁇

**Not quite . . .**

Have you read Alessandro Manzetti's Eden Underground? Another snake, another tree, another Eve. A surreal journey into obsessions and aberrations of the modern world and the darker side, which often takes control of the situation. Winner of the 2014 Bram Stoker Award for Superior Achievement in Poetry.

**If you enjoyed this book, we're certain you'll also like the following Crystal Lake titles:**

*The Third Twin—A Dark Psychological Thriller*—Some things should never be bred . . . Amid tribulation, death, madness, and institutionalization, a father fights against a scientist's bloody bid to breed a theoretical third twin.

*Embers: A Collection of Dark Fiction* by Kenneth W. Cain—These short speculative stories are the smoldering remains of a fire, the fiery bits meant to ignite the mind with slow-burning imagery and haunting details. These are the slow burning embers of Cain's soul.

*Aletheia: A Supernatural Thriller* by J.S. Breukelaar—A tale of that most human of monsters—memory—Aletheia is part ghost story, part love story, a novel about the damage done, and the damage yet to come. About terror itself. Not only for what lies ahead, but also for what we think we have left behind.

*Beatrice Beecham's Cryptic Crypt* by Dave Jeffery—The fate of the world rests in the hands of four dysfunctional teenagers and a bunch of oddball adults. What could possibly go wrong?

*Visions of the Mutant Rain Forest*—the solo and collaborative stories and poems of Robert Frazier and Bruce Boston's exploration of the Mutant Rain Forest.

*The Final Reconciliation* by Todd Keisling - Thirty years ago, a progressive rock band called The Yellow Kings began recording what would become their first and final album. Titled "The Final Reconciliation," the album was expected to usher in a new renaissance of heavy metal, but it was shelved following a tragic concert that left all but one dead. It's the survivor shares the shocking truth.

*Where the Dead Go to Die* by Mark Allan Gunnells and Aaron Dries—Post-infection Chicago. Christmas. There are monsters in this world. And they used to be us. Now it's time to euthanize to survive in a hospice where Emily, a woman haunted by her past, only wants to do her job and be the best mother possible. But it won't be long before that snow-speckled ground will be salted by blood.

*Gutted: Beautiful Horror Stories*—An anthology of dark fiction that explores the beauty at the very heart of darkness. Featuring horror's most celebrated voices: Clive Barker, Neil Gaiman, Ramsey Campbell, Paul Tremblay, John F.D. Taff, Lisa Mannetti, Damien Angelica Walters, Josh Malerman, Christopher Coake, Mercedes M. Yardley, Brian Kirk, Stephanie M. Wytovich, Amanda Gowin, Richard Thomas, Maria Alexander, and Kevin Lucia.

*Tribulations* by Richard Thomas—In the third short story collection by Richard Thomas, *Tribulations*, these stories cover a wide range of dark fiction—from fantasy, science fiction and horror, to magical realism, neo-noir, and transgressive fiction. The common thread that weaves these tragic tales together is suffering and sorrow, and the ways we emerge from such heartbreak stronger, more appreciative of what we have left—a spark of hope enough to guide us though the valley of death.

*The Dark at the End of the Tunnel* by Taylor Grant—Offered for the first time in a collected format, this selection features ten gripping and darkly imaginative stories by Taylor Grant, a Bram Stoker Award ® nominated author and rising star in the suspense and horror genres. Grant exposes the terrors that hide beneath the surface of our ordinary world, behind people's masks of normalcy, and lurking in the shadows at the farthest reaches of the universe.

**If you ever thought of becoming an author, we recommend these non-fiction titles:**

*Horror 101: The Way Forward*—A comprehensive overview of the Horror fiction genre and career opportunities available to established and aspiring authors, including Jack Ketchum, Graham Masterton, Edward Lee, Lisa Morton, Ellen Datlow, Ramsey Campbell, and many more.

*Horror 201: The Silver Scream Vol.1 and Vol.2*—A must read for anyone interested in the horror film industry. Includes interviews and essays by Wes Craven, John Carpenter, George A. Romero, Mick Garris, and dozens more. Now available in a special paperback edition.

*Modern Mythmakers: 35 interviews with Horror and Science Fiction Writers and Filmmakers* by Michael McCarty—Ever wanted to hang out with legends like Ray Bradbury, Richard Matheson, and Dean Koontz? Modern Mythmakers is your chance to hear fun anecdotes and career advice from authors and filmmakers like Forrest J. Ackerman, Ray Bradbury, Ramsey Campbell, John Carpenter, Dan Curtis, Elvira, Neil Gaiman, Mick Garris, Laurell K. Hamilton, Jack Ketchum, Dean Koontz, Graham Masterton, Richard Matheson, John Russo, William F. Nolan, John Saul, Peter Straub, and many more.

*Writers On Writing: An Author's Guide*—Your favorite authors share their secrets in the ultimate guide to becoming and being and author. Writers On Writing is an eBook series with original 'On Writing' essays by writing professionals.

**Or check out other Crystal Lake Publishing books for Tales from The Darkest Depths.**

# ABOUT THE AUTHOR

Alessandro Manzetti is a Bram Stoker Award-winning author, editor, and translator of horror fiction and dark poetry whose work has been published extensively in Italian, including novels, short and long fiction, poetry, essays, and collections. English publications include his collections *The Garden of Delight, The Massacre of the Mermaids, The Monster, the Bad and the Ugly* (with Paolo Di Orazio), *Dark Gates* (with Paolo Di Orazio), *Stockholm Syndrome* (with Stefano Fantelli), and the poetry collections *Eden Underground* (Bram Stoker Award 2015 winner), *Sacrificial Nights* (with Bruce Boston, Bram Stoker Award 2016 nominee), and *Venus Intervention* (with Corrine de Winter, Bram Stoker Award 2014 nominee). He edited the anthology *The Beauty of Death* (Bram Stoker Award 2016 nominee)

His stories and poems have appeared in Italian, USA, and UK magazines, such as *Dark Moon Digest, The Horror Zine, Disturbed Digest, Illumen, Devolution Z, Recompose, Polu Texni,* and anthologies, such as *Bones III, Rhysling Anthology* (2015, 2016, 2017), *HWA Poetry Showcase vol. 3, The Beauty of Death, Best Hardcore Horror of the Year vol. 2, Mar Dulce, I Sogni del Diavolo, Danze Eretiche vol. 2, Il Buio Dentro,* and many others.

He has translated works by Ramsey Campbell, Richard Laymon, Poppy Z. Brite, Edward Lee, Graham Masterton, Gary Braunbeck, Gene O'Neill, Lisa Morton, and Lucy Snyder. He is the owner and editor-in-chief of Independent Legions Publishing and is on the Horror Writers Assocation Board of Trustees.

Website: www.battiago.com

Hi, readers. It makes our day to know you reached the end of our book. Thank you so much. This is why we do what we do every single day.

Whether you found the book good or great, we'd love to hear what you thought. Please take a moment to leave a review on Amazon, Goodreads, or anywhere else readers visit. Reviews go a long way to helping a book sell, and will help us to continue publishing quality books.

Thank you again for taking the time to journey with Crystal Lake Publishing.

We are also on . . .

Website
http://www.crystallakepub.com/

Books
http://www.crystallakepub.com/book-table/

Blog
http://www.crystallakepub.com/blog-2/

Newsletter
http://eepurl.com/xfuKP

Instagram
https://www.instagram.com/crystal_lake_publishing/

Patreon
https://www.patreon.com/CLP

YouTube
https://www.youtube.com/c/CrystalLakePublishing

Twitter
https://twitter.com/crystallakepub

Facebook page
https://www.facebook.com/Crystallakepublishing/

Google+
https://plus.google.com/u/1/107478350897139952572

Pinterest
https://za.pinterest.com/crystallakepub/

Tumblr
https://www.tumblr.com/blog/crystal-lake-publishing

**We'd love to hear from you.**

With unmatched success since 2012, Crystal Lake Publishing has quickly become one of the world's leading indie publishers of Mystery, Thriller, and Suspense books with a Dark Fiction edge.

Crystal Lake Publishing puts integrity, honor, and respect at the forefront of our operations.

We strive for each book and outreach program that's launched to not only entertain and touch or comment on issues that affect our readers, but also to strengthen and support the Dark Fiction field and its authors.

Not only do we publish authors who are legends in the field and as hardworking as us, but we look for men and women who care about their readers and fellow human beings. We only publish the very best Dark Fiction, and look forward to launching many new careers.

We strive to know each and every one of our readers while building personal relationships with our authors, reviewers, bloggers, podcasters, bookstores, and libraries.

Crystal Lake Publishing is and will always be a beacon of what passion and dedication, combined with overwhelming teamwork and respect, can accomplish: unique fiction you can't find anywhere else.

We do not just publish books, we present you worlds within your world, doors within your mind from talented authors who sacrifice so much for a moment of your time.

This is what we believe in. What we stand for. This will be our legacy.

Welcome to Crystal Lake Publishing.

We hope you enjoyed this title. If so, we'd be grateful if you could leave a review on your blog or any of the other websites and outlets open to book reviews. Reviews are like gold to writers and publishers, since word-of-mouth is and will always be the best way to market a great book. And remember to keep an eye out for more of our books.

THANK YOU FOR PURCHASING THIS BOOK

CPSIA information can be obtained
at www.ICGtesting.com
Printed in the USA
LVHW050902140122
708387LV00014B/1141